Word

Nowhere

Lianne Neeson

BookLeaf
Publishing

India | USA | UK

Presentation by *BookLeaf Publishing*

Web: www.bookleafpub.com

E-mail: info@bookleafpub.com

ISBN: 9789360941116

First edition 2024

DEDICATION

For Daddy

Mirror Image

I look at the girl in the mirror
And I wonder what do you see?
Am I a reflection of you
Or are you just a reflection of me?
Is your world combined to the mirror
Or is there a beyond to explore?
We're only ever face to face
And I'd like to know a lot more
I feel we share more than strangers
Though we've never exchanged a word
I've sung and screamed at you sometimes
I wonder if you heard
At times I think you are beautiful
Sometimes I can't stand your face
I've thrown things to try and erase you
But often wanted to take your place
I've seen you happy and sad
Watched as you smile or cry
Wanted to give you reassurance
Desperate to ask you why
Our lives clearly run parallel
As you're everywhere I turn
I feel the need to interrogate you
There's so much about you to learn
I wonder if i look inwards

Will the answers all be there
Would our souls reflect the same
Or is it just a face that we share?

She

There is a she inside of me
She is without a mask
No filter on her voice
Untamed
I am the only one that knows she
Yet she is not lonely
She is carefree
Unfettered by the constraints that bind me to
conform
She does not worry if her words offend
She dances to a tune no one else can hear
She is unapologetic for her opinions
She is what I wish I could be
The fire in her heart burns so bright, it is
reflected in her eyes
And sometimes spills from her mouth
There are no consequences she fears
None to hold her back
She is the rebel I was born to be
Before I was raised to be me

Going Grey

I stand at the mirror and stare at my face
Not sure when it started but I want out of this
race
The rush to get older all wrinkled and grey
When did 17 get so far away?
I've loved my life and lived it well
Now when I look in the mirror it's starting to tell
There's hair starting to sprout all over my chin
And when I give a smile, it's more wrinkles than
grin
When I take off my bra, my boobs hit my knees
I'd like to start over again now please
There are things I'd tell my younger self
Now that i'm older they'd really have helped
I'd drink more water, less nights on the town
My skin would be tighter, less lines when I
frown
Crisps, chocolate and cake there's be less of that
Then my bum might be shapely, my tummy less
fat
I'd tell me to l listen when they say work hard at
school
Get a good job instead of playing the fool
They do say that hindsight is a wonderful thing

But what of the memories those bad habits
bring?
The nights that we laughed and danced 'til we
dropped
The detentions at school for the lessons we
hopped
Crying over a boy with a tub of ice cream
Or burgers and crisps as we cheered on our team
If the memories are what has made my hair grey
Then I'm all up for more and I'll lead the way!

Abigail

She roars like a lion
Quiet as a mouse
Knows she is beautiful
Still full of self doubt
She is book smart
She is silly
Independent
Still needs me
Thinks she is grown
Still such a child
She is sometimes meek
More often she's wild
A contradiction in terms
I can't help but love her
She is part of my soul
Please meet my daughter

No More Words

I'm meant to be writing a poem or two
Something I'd normally find easy to do
Today my mind is a complete dead end
Nothing to say, no words to lend
Instead of writing my pen draws a star
My name three different ways and doodles a car
Where can I start, how to begin?
I just need a word, a person, a thing
Something that can stand as my muse
Or better yet some outlandish views
Things that amuse, things that annoy
Things people hate or that bring them joy
Alas today it isn't to be
All of those things are avoiding me
So I sit here and scribble, doodle and draw
Until the words appear like they did before

Indestructible

We all feel indestructible
Until something knocks us down
We all know we are invincible
Until Death is hanging round
We are strong, we are survivors, we don't even
flinch
We stand our ground, live our lives and never
give an inch
Then the world tilts on it's axis and we are
hanging by a thread
Clinging on by fingertips
Consumed with fear and dread
All we know is lost; the truth is now a lie
All that made us happy now just makes us cry
We have to face reality, we were never winning
It's all been a facade, a lie we have been
spinning
We are broken, beaten, face down on the floor
Truly feels like there's nothing to get up for
anymore
The rug was pulled from under us as we looked
the other way
Distracted by the shiny, gleam of a promised
future day
Now we see the darkness that lies just beneath

As we are drowning in our sorrow, wrapped up
in our grief
Consumed by all the time we wasted, the things
we never said
Burdened by memories that won't stop replaying
in our head
But the brain plays it's game to keep us safe
from harm
So we rise up from the floor: forgetting is it's
balm
To keep us sane of mind
Memories are stored behind a blind
If we stop and think we can still feel the pain
But we are standing strong and indestructible
again!

No Dignity in Death

They said you would be dead today
But you're still holding on
They can't believe that you're still here
Saying how you must be so strong
I wished that you were dead today
Then wished that I didn't have to feel that way
This is not the way that it should be
I don't care what they say
I'm wishing this all over
So I can cry and grieve
The way that they are treating you
Is so hard to believe
I feel like I'm a murderer
As though I have conspired
To withdraw you from all sustenance
And leave you oh so tired
They say now that it won't be long
They say it's for the best
There's no quality of life, you see
It's time for you to rest
I'm worried that you are in pain
Don't want you to be frightened
They say that you know nothing now
But what if your senses are really heightened?
I'll sit and hold your hand today

Kiss your cheek and stroke your hair
I'm not going anywhere today
In case you leave whilst I'm not there
I look at all the nurses
My pain reflected in their eyes
They wish they could do more to help
But all their hands are tied
I wouldn't leave a dog like this
Torture for all involved
I find myself praying nightly now
"Please God, don't let me get old"

Let Me Grieve

The world is slippery beneath my feet
You are walking beside me, so why can't you
see?
The air is hard to breathe it gets stuck in my
lungs
My throat feels all clogged up by my tongue
My eyes are swollen shut from the buckets I've
cried
Can't pull myself together, believe me I have
tried
I don't want to wake and I can't fall asleep
Please just leave me here in my crumpled heap
I have no need for hugs and I don't hear your
words
Leave your touch for the dogs and the song for
the birds
I can't put this aside, it won't stay at bay
Can't say for how long, could be hours or days
Don't expect you to feel it feel it, I know that
you won't
But don't push me to talk, I'm begging you don't
I can't be responsible for what I might say
All of the hurt inside might end up displayed
It wouldn't be pretty and it wouldn't be meant
But I may end up broken and not only bent

Please leave me to grieve and let me be mad
Let the house go to rot, let the kids all be bad
It won't be forever of that I am sure
There will come a time I pick myself up off the floor
For now I need a safe space to be
I need to come home and just be me
It needs to be pcaceful and it needs to be calm
I need to have somewhere that will do me no harm

Still Here

Don't lose any sleep
There's nothing to fear
Please do not weep
I will always be here
You were my light and I was your laughter
Now I'm just past sleep awaiting our happy ever
after
I know you feel I have left you
That you are now alone
But how could I have gone
You are all that means home
If I could make a wish, I'd hear you laugh again
See the sparkle in your eyes, take away the pain
I'm always right beside you, so wipe away that
tear
I'm reaching out to touch you, every time you're
near
When you sit down in the evening with the cat
upon your lap
I'm settled right beside you having a little nap
My glass is held out as you pour yourself wine
Listen carefully you'll hear me asking "where's
mine?"
It may not be much but I want you to know
If I have a choice I will never go

So I am still here just out of sight
All day long and throughout the night
I'm watching over you as well as I can
For you are my woman and I was your man

Memories

Curly hair that never tamed
Handshake always strong
Same dad jokes again
Everything a song
"The best" at every sport he played
Always had the ball
Kids would cry "please Grandad"
But still he'd beat them all
Frank Sinatra on repeat
Cold beer in hand
Legs out in the sunshine
Brownest in the land
Advice on how to treat a friend
"Never shirk a bet"
"Don't go to sleep on an argument"
"Forgive but don't forget"
Money in his pocket
Every penny must be spent
Always so very generous
Then wondered where it went
I'll miss those jokes I groaned at
I'll miss trying to win that race
I'll miss the lunches in the pub
I'll miss your smiling face
I'm grateful you were there for me

With all of the above
So proud to call you daddy
And to have had your love

Burdened

If my load were lighter I'd lift yours too
If the hills weren't so steep
I'd carry you with me
If I knew I could make it
I wouldn't give up
I am bursting at my seams
Full of thoughts, anger, sadness
Overwhelmed with life
If I could empty it all I would
But I cannot burden someone else
There is no one else
The rope slowly tightens around my neck

Vows

Something borrowed
Never thought that was you
And how could I imagine
I'd be the something blue
A white gown
A ball of nerves
Promises to be mine
You were planning to be hers
Something old
How I thought I'd grow with you
Until the day I realised
She was your something new
Love has flown
The wedding bell turned to rust
My life in pieces
My heart now dust

After Narcissism

I find it hard to speak, to say what's on my mind
When I advocate for others I always find the
time
I will stand strong for them, let no one tear them
down
I fight against injustice and always stand my
ground
I won't stand for bullying nor bulldozing the
weak
Yet when it's me at stake I just can't seem to
speak
My mind is full of doubt, I'm not sure I like
myself
So how can I justify me to anybody else
I've spent so much time being consumed with
guilt
That I could not be good enough for the story
that you built
I take a stand for others, so they won't feel like
this
There's safety here in numbers; sometimes the
bullets miss
I'm pleased that you are happy, your story ended
well

Though I often find I don't recognise the fairytale you sell
I wish that I could tell it from the other side
But every time I try, my voice runs away to hide
I let you rewrite history, keep your rose tinted view
Never letting others see the person I know as you
I spent too much time blaming you for not letting me flower
I give you too much credit; you shouldn't have that power
But I find it hard to say, I cannot find the words to speak
So I will fight for others and stand up for the weak

Little Notes

I write you little notes
I send you little texts
When I try to say the words out loud all they do
is vex
In my head they sound so simple, very loud and
clear
From my mouth comes a jumble that's hard for
you to hear
So I write you little notes
Jot down what's in my brain
So I can change the wording and not make you
insane
You say that you don't read them but I'm not sure
thats true
After I have sent them you become a different
you
So I write you little notes
I scribble a little letter
In the hope that you will come to understand me
better

Shooting Star

I caught a shooting star in my hand
I caught a shooting star
It burned so bright
It lit up my life
It burned so hot
Now all I've got
Are the scars
To remember the shooting star

2 Little Boys

Two little boys all grown up to men
How I wish they could go back to little again
I miss the football, the mess, the fights
I'd never tell them but I miss the late nights
I miss being the most important girl in their life
I miss all the cuddles, I miss all the strife
They still check in with a call or a text
Normally asking when I can send money next
They are flying the nest, getting so grown
Now when I go in for a cuddle it's returned with
a moan
They have turned out well, they make me so
proud
But I miss when the house was busy and loud
I know its time to let go and wave them goodbye
Still it's hard to keep a tear from my eye
But my job is done, they are ready for life
I suppose the next step will be meeting the wife

I Stepped On A Spider

I stepped on a spider, down went my shoe
I wasn't looking but she didnt move
I didn't mean to end her life, so unfair
I wouldn't have trodden if I'd known she was there
I've wondered if she meant suicide
I've wondered were there family that cried
I've thought maybe she was evicted and sad
I've thought maybe people had her convinced she was bad
Was she exhausted having laid an egg sac
Or relaxing having got the kids off her back?
I'm grieving the spider that had her legs out in the sun
I've convinced myself we could have had fun
We could have been roomies, she'd take up no space
Could have scared unwanted guests by just showing her face
We could have gone out for walks in the park
Sat up knitting and weaving when it got dark
But I stepped on the spider and she is no more
There's bits on my shoe and more on the floor
Tonight as I sit on the sofa watching TV
I can feel lots of eyes staring at me

There's some on the ceiling some on the wall
As I turn my head I spy more coming down the
hall
Spiders, spiders everywhere
I think it's me they came to scare
The spider I stepped on did have descendants
And here they come seeking their vengeance

Puppy Love

Get a puppy they say, it will be fun they said
Now I'm looking online and losing my head
A small one? A big one? Long haired or short?
There are too many options, this requires some
thought
"Please mum, we'll feed it and take it for walks"
"Have you seen the cost?" my husband baulks
We're looking for something gentle and good
Easy to train not too fussy about food
A Labrador seems like the perfect choice
Now which do we want a girl or a boy?
A yellow, a chocolate or one that is black?
And what shall we call it Monty or Jack?
We decide on a red one, he is the most
handsome pup
Though he was born blind so not having much
luck
Nobody wants him, the last of his litter
But the vet says he has rarely seen a dog fitter
He also advises he will want a pal
To help him when he gets out and about
So back to the search for another puppy
Another dog to train, lucky old me
We take Monty with us to search for his friend
Litter after litter when will this end?

He finds one eventually, it's love at first sight
The race round the garden with an occasional play fight
"We'll take her she seems like a perfect match"
Although she's a silver not considered up to scratch
2 pups in the house is chaos and mess
They've chewed all the skirtings, our shoes and my dress
They wake up at 5 wanting breakfast and fuss
It's al down to me, no longer to us
He is sneaky and scatty, a lovable cad
While she is calm and chilled the best dog I ever had
I've torn out my hair and rued the day
that someone convinced me to let 2 puppies stay
But when it really matters and I'm collapsed in a huddle
There's nothing better than a Labrador cuddle
They may steal our socks, our slippers, a whole box of tarts
But what really matters is the stealing of hearts
One wag of a tail and I can't stay mad
When it comes to these pups I've got it bad!

Eco Warriors (written for my daughter to take to school for 'eco club')

"Eco Warriors?" The say it's not cool to be green
But it's cool to dump rubbish even though its
obscene
The Earth has sustained us for thousands of
years
But we have polluted it, ignored all it's tears
We have wasted resources hand over fist
Too lazy to change but soon they'll be missed
Reuse recycle this should be the way
But everyone thinks it can wait one more day
You're only one person you can't do it all
But we should all do our bit, no matter how
small
Sorting the rubbish that could be your thing
Make sure the recycling is in the right bin
When brushing your teeth turn off the tap
When you drink from a bottle don't drop the cap
Try walking to school and save your bus fare
Help the next generation to breathe clean air
If we don't start now we will watch the world
burn

There'll be nothing left when it's our children's
turn
We've raped and pillaged our planet too long
We need to stand up, we need to be strong
It's time to say stop this isn't the way
It's time now for change, no more delay
We can no longer worry what others think
This attitude clearly is starting to stink
We need to make plans, we need to plant trees
Before the whole of humanity is down on it's
knees
No longer in others can we place our trust
Change is needed and it must come from us!

Love in a Premier Inn

I woke up this morning and I had forgotten
But this is what happens when you drink until rotten
Some wine with dinner you eagerly pour
Then it's 3 in the morning and you're on bottle four
It's a girly weekend in a Premier Inn
The bar's looking fab
But so is the gin
The plan is to go out and paint the town red
But we've both drunk too much since that was said
So we sit at our table and pour one more glass
And the single one says "Cor, look at that arse!"
She's off to the bar "now strut" you joke
She obviously listened as she is snogging that bloke!
What happened next is the bit that has vanished
The embarrassing conversations my brain chose to banish
I know I woke up to a knock on the door
Hadn't made it to bed, was asleep on the floor
I'd gone into our bedroom to nip to the loo
Shut the door and locked her out, oops!
I had left them outside saying goodbyes

Sent a goodnight text then closed my eyes
Got up in the morning, went for something to eat
Lo and behold who should we meet
He'd waited to see her to bid her farewell
He promised to call, suppose time will tell
They don't live close but he has a car
And if it's true love is it ever too far?
As for me through all this brain fog
I can't wait to get home to hubby and dog!

Internet Dating

Looking through profiles, this could take all
night
Left, left, left, oh but that one's a right!
Oh help, it's a match, now what do I do?
It's ok he's typing, just follow the mood
"Hi How are you?"
"Good thanks. How are you?"
Well that's the best conversation that I ever had
Why does dating like this leave me so sad?
Quick say something clever, funny or rude?
Just not too intellectual, stupid or lewd
Can't think on my feet, have nothing to say
Though he's not deterred, sends pics anyway
There's one of him smiling
This one's a bit silly
Here's one with shirt off
Oh God, no not his willy!
What have I signed up to? This isn't for me
Quick unmatched, now block him
Will they refund my fee?
Still looking for a prince and swiping through
frogs
Yes I care if you're married (oh and if you like
dogs)
The answers I'm seeking don't seem to be here

But I'll agree to a date and swallow my fear
Turn up to a bar wonder if you're the one
Hopeful tonight will be lots of fun
You sent me a photo and that looks like you
But you said 5'11 and he's 5'2
We had a laugh, it went ok
Arranged our next one for today
All dressed up to go on our date
You send a text, you're running late
I say lets leave it, another time, don't worry
You reply "lets just stay in, have a curry"
I should have insisted on another time instead
Because you come to my house all ready for bed
In Star Wars pyjamas at my house at 10
Then wondering why I don't want to see you
again
There were 3 months with one that seemed a
good choice
Until he suddenly developed a baby voice
The one who was studying law
But forgot to mention he was a terrible bore
The one who wanted to hold my hand
But only for a one night stand
The one whose hobby was going for a walk
Didn't mention he was following girls he liked to
stalk
One likes to read, one likes to cook
One likes to travel, they all have a hook
I've been on Bumble, Tinder and Hinge

But I don't want to send pics of my minge!
I've recently considered Christian Mingle
But honestly maybe I'm better off single!

Milton Keynes UK
Ingram Content Group UK Ltd.
UKHW020743280424
441877UK00005B/17

9 789360 941116